Agile Development in .NET

Agile Development

in

.NET

DAN HERMES

Kilimanjaro Publishing

Kilimanjaro Publishing
Boston, Massachusetts 02130

ISBN: 978-1-4923-2796-7

*

For info about Dan Hermes' consulting
and speaking services, or to subscribe
to the free e-newsletter, visit:
http://www.lexiconsystemsinc.com
or email Dan at:
dan@lexiconsystemsinc.com

Visit Dan's blog at:
http://www.itshopkeeping.com

Table of Contents

Overview

Software development is important to many of us, so we strive to find better ways to do it.

In the late 20th century we spent a great deal of time and money developing requirements and specifications, thinking through each case and documenting possible uses and outcomes. We would plan a glorious plan before beginning development.

Wait, that never actually happened.

Instead, we were given a few ideas to go on, then ran to the computer and wrote some code. The Waterfall ideal of design before coding was seldom a reality. Even when there was time to plan, the design had changed so drastically by the time we began coding that it seemed like the time spent planning was wasted. In the end, we would usually have to rewrite it anyway.

What we learned was this: requirements, specification, coding, and design are not separable. Though they can be distanced for a time by process and habit, we are eventually forced to work in a cyclical fashion, reworking the design as the coding unfolds and changing the requirements as the code reveals truths previously unknown. We learned that software development is not like a track relay race where the analyst completes their laps then passes the baton to the developer. We learned that development works more like an automobile race, where each of the four tires must rest firmly on the changing terrain at all times: requirements, specifications, design, and code. The user needs must steer the vehicle, but it can also be propelled by the technical design and coding discoveries in directions that may not have been clear by requirements and specifications alone. We learned that we must design and build less code more quickly, with tighter feedback loops with the users and business stakeholders.

These lessons led us to Agile.

Implementations of the Agile Manifesto have led to tighter and faster design and coding cycles with more frequent user feedback. These new cycles result in new challenges:

> How to keep a team in sync at high speed?
> How to keep up with testing?
> How to implement super-fast releases?
> How to keep the code from becoming a mess?

Strategies have evolved to deal with each of these challenges. **Scrum** addresses the team problem with a codified approach to requirements gathering, team interaction, project schedule, and software acceptance. With the help of **Behavior-Driven Development (BDD)**, user stories provide lightweight requirements and a specification framework. Implementing user acceptance tests and having the customer and product owner on-site both offer quick feedback on completed work. Extreme Programming (XP) offers solutions to cover the other bases: **Test-Driven Development (TDD)** stepped in to tackle the testing issue, slimming down the QA step and bringing testing responsibilities back to the developers who implements them the way they know best – in the code. The release problem is resolved by **Continuous Integration (CI)**, allowing code changes to flow into production as quickly as the team can produce them. Then how to avoid sprint-induced spaghetti code? **Refactoring**, the steady and continuous reorganization of code, keeps it pruned, organized, and under control. **Design patterns** provide direction for developers to follow while they refactor.

Microsoft Visual Studio .NET and Team Foundation Server (TFS) provide ways to help us do all these things, the Agile way. For each of these topics we'll explore these questions:

- Why are these ideas important?
- How do Visual Studio and TFS help us to be agile?
- What are some third party alternatives?
- How do you get a team started?

AGILE TIPS

Be customer-centric

Welcome changing requirements

Deliver working software frequently

Agile and Scrum

The Agile Manifesto was laid out in February, 2001 at The Lodge at Snow-bird ski resort in Utah by an informal group of software developers who shared a passion for innovation and concern about current methodologies. These are the core tenets:

- Individuals and interactions over processes and tools
- Working software over comprehensive documentation
- Customer collaboration over contract negotiation
- Responding to change over following a plan

A manifesto is useful only if it leads to action. The Agile Manifesto has birthed dozens of methodologies, tools, and approaches. For the purposes of .NET development, those covered in this book are the ones that are most prevalent today in .NET development circles, software shops, and IT departments.

It is a mistake to think that Agile is a merely project management meth-odology or worse, a buzzword. Agile is a philosophy, a body of knowledge, an understanding, and experience passed through the 20th century into the present. It is, in its small way, wisdom of the ages. It's also a pendulum swing, away from a heavyweight life cycle development process with lots of front-end planning, towards a lighter-weight process with less planning and more coding, and more interaction between the most important ele-ments in software development: people.

SCRUM

A departure from traditional hierarchical project management and Waterfall life cycle, Scrum empowers the Team with a focus on delivering quick results with minimal overhead. A Scrum Team consists of a Scrum Master, a Product Owner, and everyone else who actually does the work. Those who do not do the work are not on the team – they are stakeholders. The Product Owner meets with the stakeholders to prepare a list of work to be done, the Product Backlog, in the form of brief synopsis of requirements called User Stories. This is brought to a Sprint Planning Meeting where the Team decides what work they can commit to for the next functional release. Those who do not do the work do not attend the Sprint Planning Meeting. The period where the Team works toward the next release is called a Sprint, generally lasting thirty days. Once the Sprint begins, Backlog items are frozen, both in number and in content. Changes to these commitments can lead to the termination of the Sprint. The Team and the stakeholders are therefore encouraged to complete the Sprint as committed to.

Since Agile means people over process, it is critical for the people to communicate. Scrum mandates Daily Scrum Meetings, generally fifteen minutes long. Each team member answers three questions:

1) What did they do since the last Daily Scrum Meeting?
2) What will they do before the next one?
3) What impedes them from performing their work as effectively as possible?

The results of a Sprint are presented at a Sprint Review Meeting to the Product Owner and stakeholders. Reflection on the Sprint happens in a post-mortem Sprint Retrospective Meeting for the Team where the Team discusses ideas for improvement on the next Sprint.

That's Scrum in a nutshell.

I encourage you to read a few of the best books on Agile/Scrum methodology before undertaking a sincere effort yourself, or to just hone your Agile skills. Check out the sources in the back of this book. The key authors are Ken Schwaber, Jeff Sutherland, Robert C. Martin, Alistair Cockburn, and Kent Beck.

TOOLS

A central Agile tenet states "Individuals and interactions over processes and tools". Even so, a team needs tools. Here are a few that help Scrum play well with .NET development:

TFS Scrum Template in Visual Studio

This template provides work items, reporting, and Sprint Backlog integrated into Visual Studio for TFS. Teams can track their work items' priority, status, and backlog, as well as create custom reports.

Team Explorer:

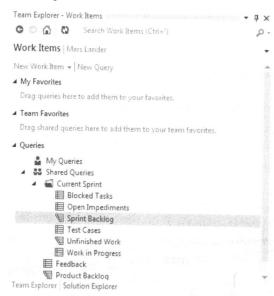

Sprint Backlog:

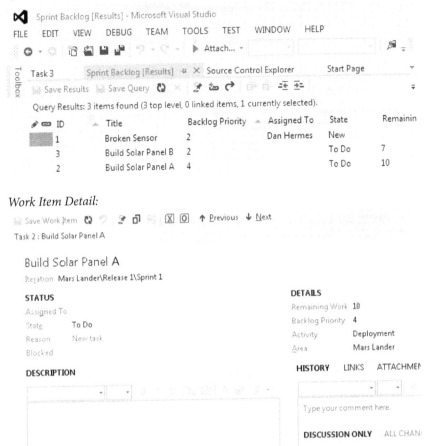

Work Item Detail:

Team Foundation Service

This TFS web component provides a graphics interface to these Scrum productivity tools, sporting a Kanban board for organizing the Product Backlog and a team dashboard for quick access to Burndown Charts.

Kanban Boards:

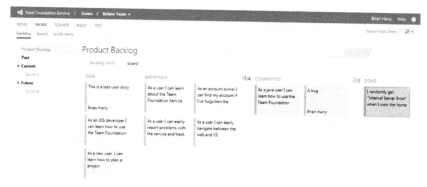

Team Web Access:

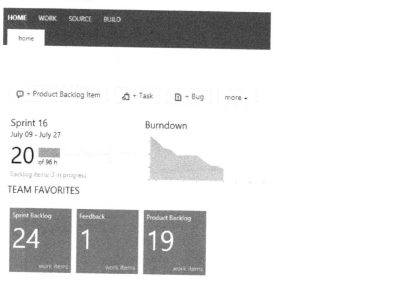

Take time to reflect, tune, adapt, and improve

Burndown Charts:

(SQL Server Reporting Services is required for this feature)

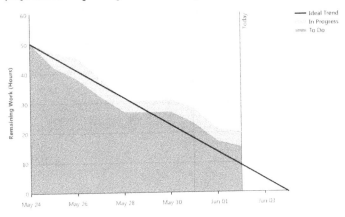

Features by TFS License

Many of the Agile features in TFS are tied to paid licensing. Here are the options for VS 2012:

Limited – no TFS Client Access License (CAL) required
- View My Work Items

Standard – TFS CAL required
- View All Work Items
- Standard Features
- Agile Boards

Full – VS Ultimate, Premium, or Test Professional
- Backlog and Sprint Planning Tools
- Request and Manage Feedback
- PowerPoint Storyboarding
- Code Review

What are the .NET-compatible alternatives?

Urban Turtle and Eylean are eye-catching Agile application platforms for TFS with add-ons for backlog prioritization, release and sprint planning, and task monitoring.

Urban Turtle offers Product Management, Agile Dashboard, Product Backlog, Sprint Backlog, and Estimation Board:

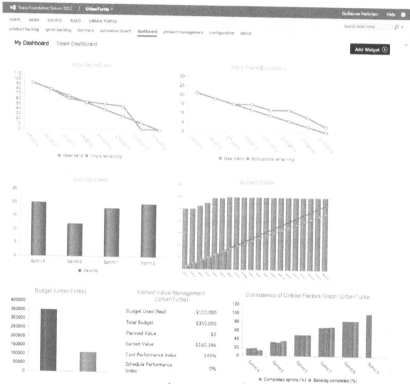

Image courtesy of Urban Turtle, http://urbanturtle.com/

Eylean has Kanban, Scrum board, time tracking, and reporting.

Eylean Assignments:

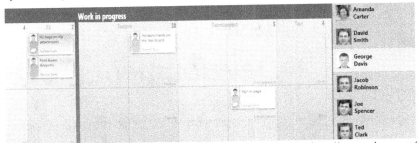

Image courtesy of Eylean by Prewise, http://www.eylean.com/

Eylean Kanban Board:

Image courtesy of Eylean by Prewise, http://www.eylean.com/

Create self-organizing teams

Test-Driven Development (TDD)

The notion of code changes can strike fear into the heart of a developer or project manager. In some cases this fear is justified. The majority of code is quite brittle and fragile, and the smallest of changes can bring an application to a grinding halt. The Agile notion of constant redesign through refactoring would be untenable without another simultaneous advance: Test-Driven Development. Constant redesign requires constant testing. The three options are:

1) The developer steps up their unit testing to include detailed functional tests every time they make a change,
2) Offload an enormous and continuous burden onto the QA team, or
3) Automate the core functional tests.

Test-Driven Development (TDD) takes the third route: automating the core functional tests.

When developers began using testing frameworks such as NUnit to develop software, they found an interesting side effect. What began as a useful way to help ensure the robustness of the code during refactoring soon took on a life of its own: Test-Driven Development now contributes to design and architecture decisions. As developers create tests they learn things about the architecture with hands-on use. It turns out that Test-Driven Development counteracts the sometimes hands-off, almost academic way in which architecture can happen. Test-Driven Development doesn't just test the code features and stories, it tests assumptions about the design as well. This implies that TDD is not just a method of verification, it can also be an approach to software architecture.

Traditionally, unit testing was carried out by the developer during and after the development of a module. In a small organization, the developer was expected to make the application entirely production-ready. In a larger organization, a team of professional testers would take the module and subject it to the full rigor of automated and manual tests. This process would be particularly thorough when the application was first created. After the first release, however, testing would be pared down to a set of regression tests, usually a much abbreviated set of tests. Quite often, even these would not be run before a new release.

Test-Driven Development reverses the traditional order and puts testing first. As developers conceive of the program structure, they create tests which the code must pass. Pure Test-Driven Development is done by writing the tests which fail before writing code to allow those tests to succeed.

> Test-Driven Development is highly effective for trivial code and code with few dependencies. Its effectiveness decreases with increased complexity and dependencies in the code.

HOW DOES .NET HELP?

The Unit Test Template in Visual Studio offers a starting point, providing a testing framework and real-time test reporting. Command-line options allow the scheduling and scripting of testing jobs. The ASP.NET MVC framework encourages testable coding practices. Testing frameworks such as NUnit, XUnit, and MBUnit are easily integrable into Visual Studio testing projects. Here's how:

The **Unit Test Template** in Visual Studio provides a testing project side-by-side with the tested code in a solution. This project implements MSTest, the default Microsoft testing framework, and the class and method attributes [TestClass] and [TestMethod]. Write test methods with an Assert to test the condition. If the Assert succeeds, the test passes.

```
using System;
using Microsoft.VisualStudio.TestTools.UnitTesting;
using FunctionLibrary;

namespace UnitTestProject1
{
    [TestClass]
    public class UnitTest1
    {
        [TestMethod]
        public void TestSum()
        {
            //Arrange
            int x = 1;
            int y = 2;

            //Act
            int Result = Functions.Sum(x, y);

            //Asset
            Assert.AreEqual(3, Result);
        }
    }
}
```

Run tests using the Test Explorer and view the results:

Arrange, Act, Assert (AAA) is a pattern used to set up and execute tests.
- Arrange – set up the unit under test
- Act – exercise the unit under test, capturing any resulting state
- Assert – verify the behavior through assertions

VSTest.Console.exe replaces MSTest in Visual Studio 2012 for command-line testing. This is useful for running automated test scripts, especially as part of a build or as scheduled jobs.

```
> vstest.console.exe [TestFileNames] [Options]
```

An example:

```
> vstest.console.exe myTestProject.dll
```

The next example shows the use of some of the options for running VSTest.Console.exe. This will run the tests in the `myTestFile.dll` file, while collecting data specified in the `Local.RunSettings` file and in an isolated process. Also, it will filter the test cases to run based in "Priority 1", and log the results to a `.trx` file:

```
> vstest.console.exe myTestFile.dll
/Settings:Local.RunSettings /InIsolation
/TestCaseFilter:"Priority=1" /Logger:trx
```

TESTING FRAMEWORKS

MSTest is the Microsoft default testing framework. There are other choices, most of them open-source. Popular testing frameworks for .NET include NUnit, xUnit.net, and MBUnit. All are implementations of XUnit.

> **XUnit** is the family name given to a group of related testing frameworks that have become widely known amongst software developers. The name is a derivation of JUnit, the first of these to be widely known.
> –*Martin Fowler*

NUnit is an open-source unit testing framework written in C#, initially ported from JUnit.

xUnit.net is an open-source unit testing tool written by the inventor of NUnit. xUnit.net is part of the ASP.NET Open-source Gallery under the Outercurve Foundation licensed under the Apache 2 license.

MbUnit is an open-source unit testing framework for .NET that is part of the Gallio Automation Platform bundle.

Watin is a .NET web-based testing framework for automating tests within browsers.

TESTABILITY

Testing frameworks provide tools to call into .NET code, but the code must be designed and architected to be receptive to testing. That is the essence of a testable application.

The **ASP.NET MVC** framework addresses some of the challenges of testability found in traditional ASP.NET by clearly separating the presentation layer from the business logic using Views and Controllers. With this approach, tests are more likely to have clear target methods. Although this is still possible in ASP.NET with disciplined coding practices and a clear architectural direction, MVC offers a built-in model for testing without much additional thought and effort on the part of the developer. Tests call Actions in the Controller layer, returning results as Models, which are object data structures. Tests can parse the resulting models and determine if the data is correct.

Models and ORM

In addition to testable code, the testability of data is also important in TDD. In general, database tables are not very testable. Non-standard and ad-hoc data objects aren't very testable either. The most testable data constructs are data object models. Classes constructed for the sole purpose of housing data offer clear ways to compare, manipulate, and verify data values during testing. This is one reason why Object Relational Mapping (ORM) is on the rise again: to support Test-Driven Development. .NET solutions include Entity Framework and NHibernate.

MOCKING

One of the biggest challenges in TDD is the lack of transparency in the behavior of objects during testing. Return values can be observed in certain situations and the object can be queried for state, but much information is lost about the objects that are called and created by the tested object.

Mock objects are wrapped around real objects and inserted into the testing process to increase the transparency of the tested application and to shed light on the behavior of the real objects therein. This practice is called mocking.

A *mock* is a wrapper around a real object that allows tracking of real method calls and input and output parameters. This wrapper is designed with expectations corresponding to the tests: Which methods does it expect to be called? What are the expected inputs? What are the expected results? A mock object is a real object wrapped by a set of tests, invoked in the course of the testing process.

> A mock is an object that knows how to check itself.
> Did I do this right? Yes, OK.
> Did I do this right? Nope.

Classical TDD vs. Mocking:
State Verification vs. Behavior Verification

Mocks enable verification of the complete behavior of the real object, including which methods were called, the input parameters, and the results. This is called *behavior verification*, an advance on the more traditional testing method called *state verification*, which checks only the return values of an object. Martin Fowler drew this important distinction between the traditional method of testing and a more complete method of testing.

State verification determines whether the tested method worked correctly by examining the state of the application after the method was called. This is used in classical TDD: the test calls the methods on real objects then examines the returned parameters for correctness.

Behavior verification checks to see if the correct calls were made in the first place. The test calls the methods on a mock object and the mock object calls the real object. The mock object verifies that the correct calls were

---

Stubs

Mocks can be confused with stubs. A *stub* (or *fake*) is a simplified imitation of a real object that returns canned responses to method calls. Sometimes we need an object to return certain values, but we don't want this call to be part of the test. Instead, we just want specific, predictable results so we can get on with the important parts of a test. Tests call stubs to emulate the response of an object for the purpose of testing another real object. Calling a stub helps a test keep focus, narrowing down the amount of code being tested.

---

made with the correct parameters and the correct results were returned. Expectations are defined, tests run, then the results are reported back to the calling test.

MOCKING FRAMEWORKS

NSubstitute is a good starter tool with a simple language and approach.

FakeItEasy is a simple tool for creating fake objects, mocks, and stubs.

Moq includes support for Linq expression trees and lambda expressions. Unusual in the sense of not using record/replay, Moq is strongly-typed and supports both interfaces and classes.

Rhino Mocks is an open-source option for .NET supporting virtual methods only. Mocking classes without virtual members are not supported. Rhino Mocks offers two syntaxes: *Record/Play* and *Arrange, Act, Assert*.

Some testers use one of the simpler tools as a standby, then switch to a more full-featured tool when the need arises.

Record/Play

Mock expectations are set up in the Record block and the test is executed in the Play/Replay block. An alternative to Arrange, Act, Assert.

Behavior-Driven Development (BDD)

Speed is immaterial if you are not clear on your destination. The flexibility and velocity afforded us by Agile methodologies is only useful if there is a clear target. Agilists argue that the only measure of success in software is a useable deliverable. That means that the software must allow the user to do something specific with it. That "something specific" is known as a User Story, and these can be defined and tested using Behavior-Driven Testing, the primary practice in Behavior-Driven Development (BDD). A relative of the Use Case, the Behavior-Driven Test defines the user action and tangible result which must take place in order for a software feature to test positive. The test follows a *Given-When-Then* paradigm called a *Step Definition*. Here's the format:

- Given (preconditions)
- When (event occurs)
- Then (a testable outcome is achieved)

An example:

- **Given** there is coffee left in the store and I have paid the cashier $5 plus tip
- **When** I stand in line in front of the barista's counter
- **Then** I should be served a coffee

Cucumber is a Ruby-based open-source tool for running automated acceptance tests written in a Behavior-Driven Development style.

The parser for Cucumber is **Gherkin**, a BDD language fueled by the open-source Gherkin Project. Gherkin is where step definitions, Given-When-Then (GWT), come from. Ruby scripts are used to build upon the GWT features to create cases and conditionals.

BDD IN .NET

There is no Microsoft solution for Behavior-Driven Development at this time, so here are a few open-source tools for .NET, all descended from or related to Cucumber:

SpecFlow is a non-Ruby .NET product which ties user stories into automated tests, a concept called executable specifications. It uses the same Gherkin parser as Cucumber and is integrated with Visual Studio, TFS, and MSBuild, as well as NUnit, MSTest, xUnit.Net, and MbUnit.

Cuke4Nuke is a Ruby-based project that hosts your step definitions in a .NET application connecting to Cucumber over a TCP/IP connection.

IronRuby is a .NET implementation of Ruby that runs Cucumber.

Businesspeople and developers must work together daily

Continuous Integration (CI)

The thing about Agile is that *all* steps need to be agile, not just development, in order to keep things moving. We have discussed agility in testing, architecture, and development. It is natural to require agility in the release process as well.

There was a time when a release to production of a fully developed and tested enterprise application could take weeks, even months. Between code merges, branch conflicts, out of sync code bases, and configuration issues, these infrequent events could make every release feel as painful as the first.

The speed of Agile development makes such delays unworkable.

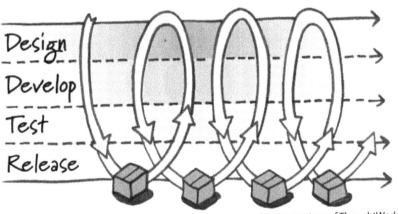

Image courtesy of ThoughtWorks

To keep pace with the Sprints, Agile releases need to move as fast and as smoothly as possible. We need releases to happen in tandem with each Sprint, so there's no time for a lengthy merge step. That means the merging of code must happen continuously. Thus: Continuous Integration.

CI FRAMEWORKS

Team Foundation Server (TFS) is Microsoft's full-featured Continuous Integration option. Set up a central TFS build server with shared drop/staging folders to receive compiled executables and log files. Builds take place on this server as required: upon each successful merge and check-in, at intermittent days and times, or manually.

TeamCity is a Java-based build management and continuous integration server from JetBrains. It integrates with Team Foundation Server and other version control systems such as Subversion as well as NUnit, MSTest, MSBuild, NAnt, MSpec, xUnit, and all Gallio-based frameworks.

Cruisecontrol.NET provides an open-source framework for CI with a build status dashboard and web-based build reporting. A build loop feeds real-time status of check-ins and the build to the dashboard and reports. This product is integrated with Visual Studio, NAnt, Msbuild, Nunit, and others. It can be run as a console application or as a Windows service and offers plug-ins to many additional apps such as email integration. This compiler uses the core .NET compilation executables: devenv.exe and msbuild.exe.

> My general rule of thumb is that every developer should commit to the repository every day.
> –Martin Fowler

BUILD SCRIPTING

Build scripting is a programming tool for creating and managing builds. It empowers developers and release engineers to take control of the build through automation, flexible releases, and conditional construction of builds using code. It also permits integration with TDD and BDD tools. Most .NET build scripts are descended from the UNIX *make* command.

MSBuild is Microsoft's default build scripting language, integrated with Visual Studio, a .NET implementation of NAnt. TFS relies heavily on MSBuild.

NAnt is the open-source .NET implementation of Apache Ant. Cross-platform, supporting Linux and Mono, NAnt is useful for installing a web site to multiple targets (i.e., Linux Apache and Windows IIS). NAnt provides integration with NUnit for running unit tests as part of the build, and with NDoc for producing documentation.

Our measure of success: working software

Maintain a constant pace indefinitely

Have face-to-face conversations

Refactoring to Design Patterns

Coding, testing, and releasing at breakneck speed…what could go wrong?

TECHNICAL DEBT

Constant changes to a system lead to disorganized code, which is fragile and costly to maintain. This has been referred to as spaghetti code and code rot. Each feature we add without spending an equal amount of time reorganizing the code accrues some measure of *technical debt*. Agile's fast pace and change-orientation raises the risk of bringing about the early demise of a system. So how do we pay off that debt before it accrues?

The life cycle of software is well-established: enhance the code until it becomes unmaintainable then build a new system and repeat the cycle. Though this cycle is unavoidable, Agile coding techniques counter the erosion of design and can lengthen the life span of a system, keep it in better working order while in use, and lower the costs of maintaining it.

As new features are added and bugs fixed, the developers reorganize code to absorb all those changes. The reorganization is informed by industry norms, providing developers with tried-and-true approaches to solve common problems. Refactoring happens daily, even hourly, slowing the accrual of technical debt. The norms for this discipline are *design patterns* and the coding techniques are called *refactoring*.

Pre-Agile designs directly addressed possible future changes and features. Rather than coding with specific future changes in mind, Agile architecture accounts for the present needs while providing elasticity for future growth. Extensibility is made possible through structure rather than adding unused or open-ended code to support future features.

> Design patterns provide targets for refactorings.
> –*Erich Gamma*

A FEW COMMON REFACTORINGS

Here are a few of the most common refactorings to give you a general idea of the discipline, what it's for, and why we use it. Refactoring and design patterns are as wide as they are deep, so I refer you to the many excellent sources on this subject in the back of this book for more detail and code examples.

Renaming Variables can better reflect their purpose to the reader of the code. Well-named variables can reduce the need for code comments. Self-documentation is a goal of refactoring.

> Refactoring is a technique to improve the quality of existing code. It works by applying a series of small steps, each of which changes the internal structure of the code, while maintaining its external behavior. You begin with a program that runs correctly, but is not well structured, refactoring improves its structure, making it easier to maintain and extend.
> –*Martin Fowler*

Extracting Methods is the removal of blocks of code from other blocks of code to isolate them and make them more reusable. This is akin to breaking up run-on sentences or large blocks of text into paragraphs.

Convert Array to an Object moves the code into an OOP-friendly structure that lends itself to further refactoring. Arrays are hard to refactor.

Convert Conditional to Polymorphism cuts down on unwieldy *if-then* statements which must be repeated throughout the code base. Polymorphism pushes conditional logic back into data classes and keeps the business logic handling those classes cleaner.

Simplicity

the art of maximizing the amount of work not done

is essential

VISUAL STUDIO REFACTORINGS

Visual Studio provides limited support for refactoring. Here are the Visual Studio refactorings:

- Rename
- Extract Method
- Encapsulate Field
- Extract Interface
- Remove Parameters
- Reorder Parameters

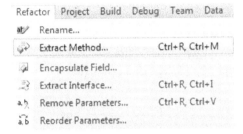

RESHARPER REFACTORINGS

The most full-featured option for refactoring within Visual Studio is the ReSharper plug-in by JetBrains. Here are the refactorings provided by ReSharper:

- Adjust Namespaces
- Change Signature (Parameters)
- Convert Abstract Class to Interface/Interface to Abstract Class
- Convert Anonymous to Named Type
- Convert Extension Method to Plain Static
- Convert Indexer (Default Property) to Method
- Convert Interface to Abstract Class

- Convert Method to Indexer (Default Property)
- Convert Method to Property
- Convert Property to Auto-Property
- Convert Property to Method(s)
- Convert Static to Extension Method
- Copy Type
- Encapsulate Field
- Extract Class
- Extract Class from Parameters
- Extract Interface
- Extract Method
- Extract Superclass
- Inline Field/Method/Variable
- Introduce Field/Parameter/Introduce Variable
- Make Method Non-Static/Non-Shared/Static/Shared
- Move Static Member
- Move String to Resource
- Move to Folder
- Move Type to Another File or Namespace/Outer Scope/ Matching Files
- Move Members Up/Down
- Rename
- Replace Constructor with Factory Method
- Safe Delete
- Transform Out Parameters to Tuple
- Use Base Type where Possible

DESIGN PATTERNS

.NET has the advantage of resting on several older technology stacks. Among those are C++ and Visual Basic. VB lent rapid application development ease to .NET and C++ provided hard-nosed coding acumen. Design patterns arose from years of C++ development in the '90s and were first documented by four developers affectionately referred to as the "Gang of Four", or the tweet-friendly acronym: GoF. Hard-won C++ lessons carry easily into the world of C# and VB.NET.

Patterns are used in manufacturing factories to help with the cutting and fabrication of products in many industries: clothes, metal, plastic components, and even silicon for CPU chips. Design patterns in software are blueprints for ways that code has worked well in certain situations for many developers in the past. As developers refactor their code to create more organized, maintainable structures, they can implement design patterns and, more commonly, combinations of design patterns. While refactoring is nothing more than moving code around, a design pattern gives that move a direction, purpose, and function.

.NET and Visual Studio do not provide tools or helpers to implement most design patterns. This is why reading, research, and hands-on practice are important in the application of design patterns in .NET. Most design patterns are implemented through manually refactoring code to utilize them, possibly through the use of a refactoring tool (such as ReSharper). Refactoring tools do not yet create or emulate design patterns. The implementation of design patterns is left entirely up to the discretion and skills of the developer.

.NET provides native support for two design patterns: Model-View-Controller (MVC) and Model-View-ViewModel (MVVM).

ASP.NET MVC Framework

Weary of unstructured and inelegant ASP.NET code, developers have opted for Microsoft's upgrade to that framework, ASP.NET MVC. Model-View-Controller is a pattern that decouples the data classes (Models) from the presentation layer (Views) from the business logic serving the application (Controllers). Data flows into the Models and is acted upon by methods within the Controllers called Actions. Views are coded in a

REST-ful style without ASP.NET baggage such as ViewState. A scripting language more elegant than ASP.NET called Razor permits client-side logic with easy access to HTML and AJAX via *helpers*. The resulting code is largely cleaner and easier to read and maintain than ASP.NET pages with code-behinds. It also lends itself naturally to Test-Driven Development, making it an obvious choice for Agile development.

WPF Model View ViewModel (MVVM) Pattern

Much in the same way that the MVC provides a more disciplined, maintainable approach to .NET development, the MVVM pattern capitalizes on one of the strongest features of desktop development: real-time data binding. The ViewModel provides an interactive data structure for the View to bind to, laid on the foundation of a pure data Model. Most enterprise Windows Presentation Foundation (WPF) development utilizes this pattern.

Epilogue

Agile is an evolved, enlightened approach to software development. Hundreds of companies have proven that Agile and Scrum can work. The jury is still out on the overall effectiveness of Test-Driven Development, Continuous Integration, and refactoring to patterns. The complexities of these practices can offset their benefits, so they must be used judiciously. Used wisely and in combination, all of these techniques provide a powerful addition to the arsenal of any developer or development shop.

I hope you found this booklet useful and I wish you luck in your journey to build better software.

Sources

Agile Principles, Patterns, and Practices in C#, Robert C. Martin, Prentice Hall, 2006.

Agile Project Management with Scrum, Ken Schwaber, Microsoft Press, 2004.

Agile Software Development Ecosystems, Jim Highsmith, Addison-Wesley Professional, 2002.

Agile Software Development, Alistair Cockburn, Addison-Wesley Professional, 2nd edition, 2006.

The Art of Unit Testing: With Examples in .Net, Roy Osherove, Manning Publications, 2009.

Clean Code: A Handbook, Robert C. Martin, Prentice Hall, 2008.

Continuous Delivery: Reliable Software Releases through Build, Test, and Deployment Automation, Jez Humble and David Farley, Addison-Wesley Professional, 2010.

Continuous Integration in .NET, Marcin Kawalerowicz, Manning Publications, 2011.

Continuous Integration: Improving Software Quality and Reducing Risk, Paul Duvall, Steve Matyas and Andrew Glover, Addison-Wesley Professional, 2007.

The Culture Game, Daniel Mezick, FreeStanding Press, 2012.

Design Patterns, Erich Gamma, Richard Helm, Ralph Johnson and John Vlissides, Addison-Wesley Professional, 1994.

Extreme Programming Explained, Kent Beck, Addison-Wesley Professional, 2nd edition, 2004.

Peopleware: Productive Projects and Teams, Tom DeMarco and Timothy Lister, Dorset House, 2nd edition, 1999.

The Power of Scrum, Jeff Sutherland, CreateSpace Independent Publishing Platform, 2011.

Pro Agile .NET Development with Scrum, Jerrel Blankenship, Matthew Bussa and Scott Millet, Apress, 2011.

Refactoring to Patterns, Joshua Kerievsky, Addison-Wesley Professional, 2004.

Refactoring: Improving the Design of Existing Code, Martin Fowler, Addison-Wesley Professional, 1999.

Visual Studio Team Foundation Server 2012: Adopting Agile Software Practices: From Backlog to Continuous Feedback, Sam Guckenheimer, Addison-Wesley Professional, 3rd edition, 2012.

ONLINE SOURCES

http://agilemanifesto.org/

http://martinfowler.com/articles.html

http://martinfowler.com/articles/mocksArentStubs.html

http://martinfowler.com/articles/newMethodology.html

About the Author

Dan Hermes is a sought-after speaker and advisor to dozens of software-building organizations, including Fidelity Investments, EDS, Blue Cross Blue Shield, TJX, and Computerworld Magazine. Mr. Hermes has over twenty-five years experience as a software management consultant, .NET architect and developer. He has taught software architecture and development at Northeastern University and Microsoft User Groups, and Microsoft Certification classes at corporate training facilities. A thought leader and innovator in several fields, Mr. Hermes is also active in the arts. His music compositions have aired on NPR. He has taught his music curriculum at Boston Conservatory. His audiovisual artwork has exhibited internationally. Cited on Forbes and Reuters, Mr. Hermes has written articles published by Media-N and MIT Press. Mr. Hermes is certified by the National Speakers Association New England (NSANE). He has served on the board of the Institute of Management Consultants New England Chapter and is currently director of Art Technology New England (ATNE). He is founder and principal of his consulting firm, Lexicon Systems, providing Microsoft .NET and Xamarin mobile development strategy nationwide.

Website: http://www.lexiconsystemsinc.com
Dan's blog is http://www.itshopkeeping.com
He can be reached by email at dan@lexiconsystemsinc.com

www.ingramcontent.com/pod-product-compliance
Lightning Source LLC
Chambersburg PA
CBHW060932050326
40689CB00013B/3054